Snakeskin Canyon

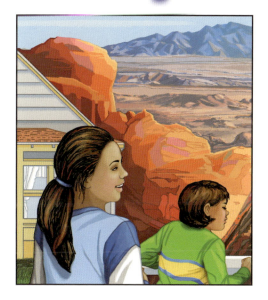

By Becky Gold
Illustrated by Diana Kizlauskas

Scott Foresman
is an imprint of

Glenview, Illinois • Boston, Massachusetts • Chandler, Arizona •
Upper Saddle River, New Jersey

Illustrations

Diana Kizlauskas.

Photographs

Every effort has been made to secure permission and provide appropriate credit for photographic material. The publisher deeply regrets any omission and pledges to correct errors called to its attention in subsequent editions.

Unless otherwise acknowledged, all photographs are the property of Pearson Education, Inc.

16 Demetrio Carrasco/©DK Images.

ISBN 13: 978-0-328-50855-6
ISBN 10:   0-328-50855-1

Copyright © by Pearson Education, Inc., or its affiliates. All rights reserved. Printed in the United States of America. This publication is protected by copyright, and permission should be obtained from the publisher prior to any prohibited reproduction, storage in a retrieval system, or transmission in any form or by any means, electronic, mechanical, photocopying, recording, or likewise. For information regarding permissions, write to Pearson Curriculum Rights & Permissions, One Lake Street, Upper Saddle River, New Jersey 07458.

Pearson® is a trademark, in the U.S. and/or in other countries, of Pearson plc or its affiliates.
Scott Foresman® is a trademark, in the U.S. and/or in other countries, of Pearson Education, Inc., or its affiliates.

6 7 8 9 10 V010 15 14 13 12

Lori just moved to Arizona.

"This place looks like the moon," she said.

"The canyons look that way. But we don't need a space suit to see them," said her cousin Julia.

"Let's go look. It will be fun!" said Julia.

Lori liked Julia. But she wasn't sure about her new home. She didn't like the name—Snakeskin Canyon. Lori hated snakes.

Lori's tire hit a rock and she lost her balance. She fell off her bike. Julia helped her.

"The ground is hard, like rock!" said Lori.

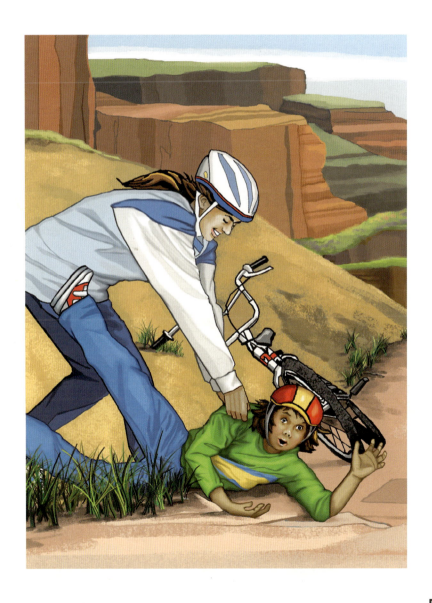

The girls rode down a hill and saw a sign.

It said: Snakeskin Nature Center.

"I visit this place all the time," said Julia.

"What animals live here?" Lori asked.
Julia replied, "Birds and snakes and …."
"Snakes?" Lori cried. Julia smiled. "Coral snakes and rattlesnakes. But don't worry. Snakes don't come near people."

"There's a story about this cave," Julia said.

"They say a miner lived here."

Lori bent down. She saw something sparkle.

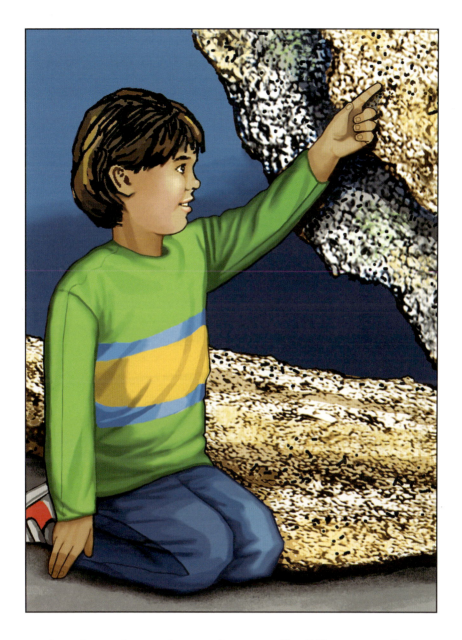

Lori pointed to the wall. Slivers of rock sparkled. "What's this?" she asked.

Julia bent beside her. "It's fool's gold. It's a rock called pyrite. It looks a bit like real gold."

Then the girls went to the nature center. They saw a snake in a big glass tank.

"Look at its rattle!" Lori said.

Soon the girls left to go home.

"The rocks are so colorful!" Lori said. Then she smiled. She saw the trees sway. She heard the wind whisper.

"I think you will like it here!" said Julia.

The Grand Canyon

There are many canyons in Arizona. Some are small and some are big. The Grand Canyon is the biggest and most famous. It is 277 miles long, 18 miles wide, and 5,000 feet deep.

Many scientists think the canyon began to form millions of years ago. They think water from the Colorado River made the canyon. Today this river still flows at the bottom of the Canyon.